OLYMPIAD WORKBOOK

INTERNATIONAL ENGLISH OLYMPIAD

01 **Learning Objectives**

02 **Multiple Choice Questions**

03 **HOTS (Achievers Section)**

04 **Model Test Paper**

05 **Answer Keys and Solutions**

06 **OMR Answer Sheet**

V&S PUBLISHERS

Published by:

V&S PUBLISHERS

F-2/16, Ansari road, Daryaganj, New Delhi-110002
☎ 23240026, 23240027 • *Fax:* 011-23240028
✉ info@vspublishers.com • ⊕ www.vspublishers.com

Online Brandstore: amazon.in/vspublishers

Regional Office : Hyderabad
5-1-707/1, Brij Bhawan (Beside Central Bank of India Lane)
Bank Street, Koti, Hyderabad - 500 095
☎ 040-24737290
✉ vspublishershyd@gmail.com

Follow us on:   

BUY OUR BOOKS FROM: AMAZON FLIPKART

© Copyright: **V&S PUBLISHERS**
ISBN 978-81-978021-6-4
New Edition

DISCLAIMER

PUBLISHER'S NOTE

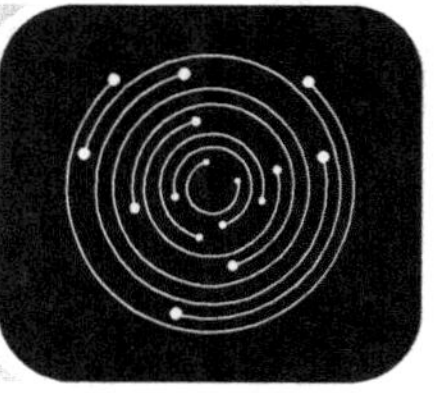

V&S Publishers has carved a significant niche in the publishing industry over the last decade, having successfully published more than 1000 titles across 9 languages spanning over 50 subject categories. Being known for the quality of content, we have built a reputation of excellence and reliability. We have consistently delivered **"Value & Substance"** to our readers, through a wide range of titles across a variety of genres covering school books, fiction and non-fiction that caters to different people from every section of the society.

The **Olympiad Guidebooks for classes 1-10** across all subjects, launched almost a decade ago, under the **GEN X Imprint**, became a go-to-source for the school students in no time, owing to their invaluable and substantive content written in a guidebook pattern,.

Having successfully sold a million copies of the same and in response to demand by both students as well as shopkeepers nationwide; we now present before you our newly launched **Olympiad Workbook Series**, designed for **classes 1-10 across 4 subjects**.

The workbooks are meticulously curated by a team of experienced educators, researchers and subject matter experts, edited by professionals and peer reviewed by teachers. The team has poured its efforts and expertise into creating a crisp and concise workbook which will help and guide the students to the path of success in Olympiad exams. The **MCQs** identified will not only help in scoring top marks in Olympiads but also inculcate a sense of deeper understanding of the subject, by way of solving **HOTS** and referring to complete solutions at the end of the book.

Here we present our new release– **OLYMPIAD WORKBOOK (IEO) CLASS–1** having following features:

- ☞ Based on the latest syllabi
- ☞ MCQs with comprehensive coverage of topics
- ☞ HOTS Questions liberally included
- ☞ A dedicated chapter on logical reasoning
- ☞ Model test paper for thorough practice
- ☞ Sample OMR sheet for real time simulation

We have made sure through our best efforts, that this workbook strictly follows the latest syllabi and patterns of the Olympiad Examination.

As **V&S Publishers** continuously strive to enhance the readability and maintain the credibility of our academic publications, we seek the support of our valuable readers in influencing and enriching the lives of future generations of students.

P.S. While every care has been taken to ensure the correctness of the content, if you come across any error, howsoever minor, do not hesitate to discuss with teachers while pointing that out to us in no uncertain terms.

We wish you all the best for your exams!

DISTINCTIVE FEATURES

CONTENTS

LEARNING OBJECTIVES

➤ Identifying words by seeing an image
➤ Jumbled words and sentences

PRACTICE EXERCISE

Form meaningful words from the following jumbled words.

For example:

SERHO

(A) HORSE
(B) ERHSO
(C) ROSEH
(D) ORSEH

1. OLWYLE

    (A) WLLOEY
    (B) YELLOW
    (C) EOLWYL
    (D) ELLWYO

2. HIFGT

    (A) GHIFT
    (B) THIFG
    (C) FIGHT
    (D) IFGTH

3. SILET

    (A) STILE
    (B) ITLES
    (C) LETIS
    (D) TILES

4. ACROYN

    (A) CRAYON
    (B) YRACON
    (C) NOCRAY
    (D) OCRAYN

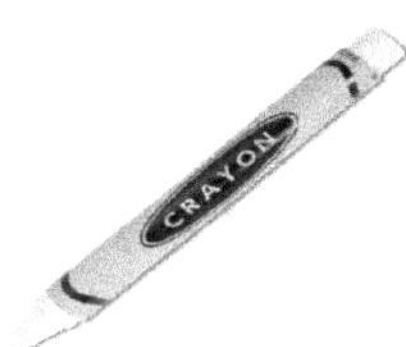

5. AGREND

    (A) RDENGA
    (B) ENGRAD
    (C) ANGERD
    (D) GARDEN

6. HACEB

    (A) CHEAB
    (B) CABEH
    (C) BEACH
    (D) ACEHB

7. OTWEL

    (A) TOWEL
    (B) WELTO
    (C) LOWTE
    (D) ETLWO

8. SELLH

    (A) LESHL
    (B) ESLHL
    (C) SHELL
    (D) ESHLL

9. JLYU
   (A) YLUJ
   (B) ULJY
   (C) JULY
   (D) YUJL

10. OGRF
   (A) GROF
   (B) ORGF
   (C) ROGF
   (D) FROG

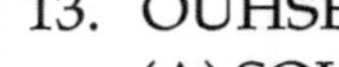

11. EGRIT
   (A) TIGER
   (B) GRTIE
   (C) REGTI
   (D) ITREG

12. ONOLBAL
   (A) LONLOAB
   (B) BALLOON
   (C) NOLOLAB
   (D) OONLLAB

13. OUHSE
   (A) SOUHE
   (B) HUSOE
   (C) EHUOS
   (D) HOUSE

14. WWDOIN
   (A) WINDOW
   (B) WODNIW
   (C) DOWWIN
   (D) NOWDIW

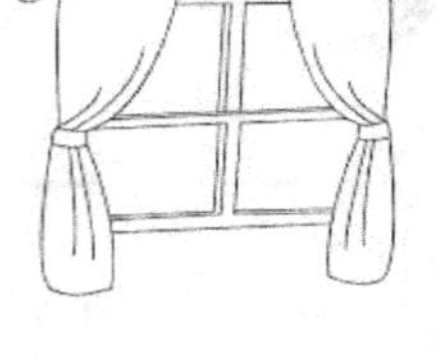

15. LPATN
   (A) PLANT
   (B) TLANP
   (C) ANTLP
   (D) LANTP

Look at the pictures and circle the correct name of the objects. The first two have been done for you.

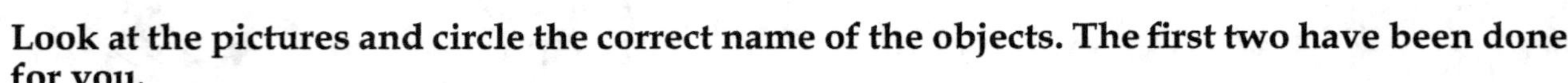

S. No.	Object	Name
16.		(A) BALL (B) APPLE *(circled)* (C) BALLOON (D) WATERMELON
17.		(A) BEAR (B) COW (C) DEER *(circled)* (D) DOG

18.		(A) BELL (B) GLASS (C) BUCKET (D) CANDLE
19.		(A) FLOWER (B) RAINBOW (C) BOW (D) ROPE
20.		(A) CANDY (B) PILLOW (C) COTTON (D) CLOWN
21.		(A) COAT (B) BAG (C) SHIRT (D) JACKET
22.		(A) ONION (B) MOUSE (C) FROG (D) RAT
23.		(A) TREES (B) FLOWERS (C) SHIPS (D) UMBRELLA

24.		(A) BAT (B) TUBE (C) BOTTLE (D) GLASS
25.		(A) SANDALS (B) SHOES (C) SLIPPERS (D) SOCKS

HOTS (ACHIEVERS SECTION)

Form meaningful words from the following jumbled words.

26. RIPZE
    (A) ZEPRI
    (B) PRIZE
    (C) EPIZR
    (D) IPRZE

27. EFET
    (A) EETF
    (B) TEEF
    (C) FEET
    (D) ETEF

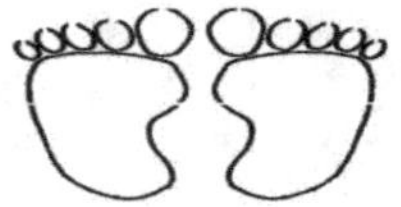

Look at the pictures and circle correct name of the objects.

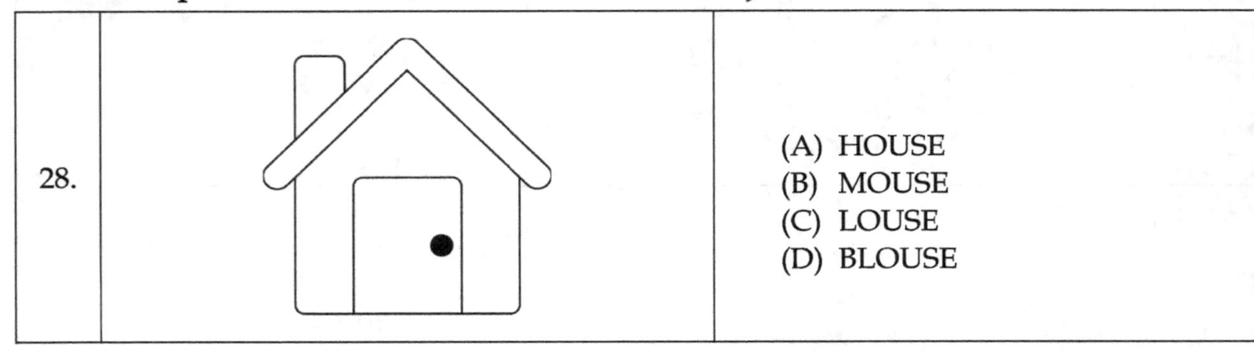

28.		(A) HOUSE (B) MOUSE (C) LOUSE (D) BLOUSE

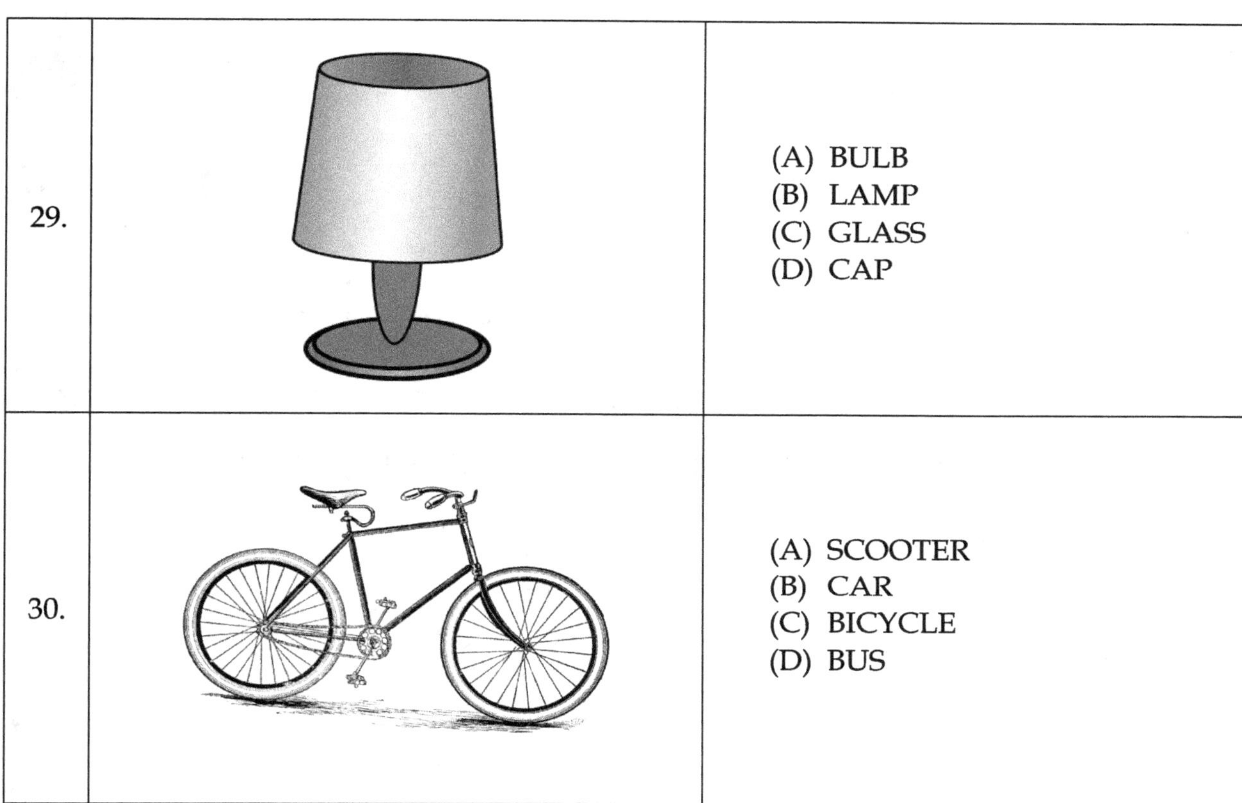

29.	(A) BULB (B) LAMP (C) GLASS (D) CAP
30.	(A) SCOOTER (B) CAR (C) BICYCLE (D) BUS

1.	Ⓐ Ⓑ Ⓒ Ⓓ	7.	Ⓐ Ⓑ Ⓒ Ⓓ	13.	Ⓐ Ⓑ Ⓒ Ⓓ	19	Ⓐ Ⓑ Ⓒ Ⓓ	25.	Ⓐ Ⓑ Ⓒ Ⓓ
2.	Ⓐ Ⓑ Ⓒ Ⓓ	8.	Ⓐ Ⓑ Ⓒ Ⓓ	14.	Ⓐ Ⓑ Ⓒ Ⓓ	20.	Ⓐ Ⓑ Ⓒ Ⓓ	26.	Ⓐ Ⓑ Ⓒ Ⓓ
3.	Ⓐ Ⓑ Ⓒ Ⓓ	9.	Ⓐ Ⓑ Ⓒ Ⓓ	15.	Ⓐ Ⓑ Ⓒ Ⓓ	21.	Ⓐ Ⓑ Ⓒ Ⓓ	27.	Ⓐ Ⓑ Ⓒ Ⓓ
4.	Ⓐ Ⓑ Ⓒ Ⓓ	10.	Ⓐ Ⓑ Ⓒ Ⓓ	16.	Ⓐ Ⓑ Ⓒ Ⓓ	22.	Ⓐ Ⓑ Ⓒ Ⓓ	28.	Ⓐ Ⓑ Ⓒ Ⓓ
5.	Ⓐ Ⓑ Ⓒ Ⓓ	11.	Ⓐ Ⓑ Ⓒ Ⓓ	17.	Ⓐ Ⓑ Ⓒ Ⓓ	23.	Ⓐ Ⓑ Ⓒ Ⓓ	29.	Ⓐ Ⓑ Ⓒ Ⓓ
6.	Ⓐ Ⓑ Ⓒ Ⓓ	12.	Ⓐ Ⓑ Ⓒ Ⓓ	18.	Ⓐ Ⓑ Ⓒ Ⓓ	24.	Ⓐ Ⓑ Ⓒ Ⓓ	30.	Ⓐ Ⓑ Ⓒ Ⓓ

WORDS AND THEIR MEANINGS

LEARNING OBJECTIVES

➤ Different words and their meanings

PRACTICE EXERCISE

Choose the word with the same meaning from the given options.

For example:

COLD
- (A) LATE
- (B) CHILLY
- (C) DRY
- (D) SHY

1. WARM
   - (A) TOASTY
   - (B) WET
   - (C) COLD
   - (D) FIRE

2. WALK
   - (A) RUN
   - (B) JUMP
   - (C) STROLL
   - (D) TALK

3. TINY
   - (A) HUGE
   - (B) TALL
   - (C) GOOD
   - (D) SMALL

4. DIRTY
   - (A) RAIN
   - (B) TIDY
   - (C) STRONG
   - (D) MESSY

5. STOP
   - (A) BREAK
   - (B) HALT
   - (C) TRIP
   - (D) SIGNAL

6. HAPPY
   - (A) GLOOMY
   - (B) SWEET
   - (C) GLAD
   - (D) BIRTHDAY

7. SICK
   - (A) ILL
   - (B) SWOLLEN
   - (C) HARD
   - (D) FEVER

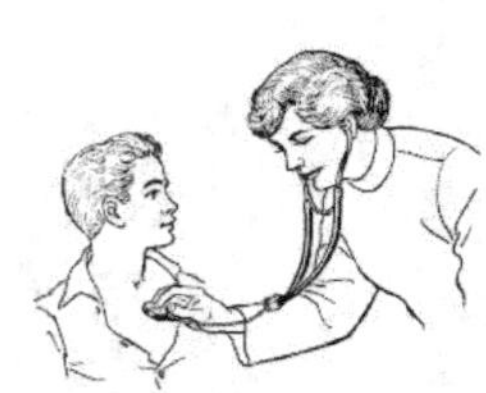

8. ANGRY
   - (A) HAPPY
   - (B) HURT
   - (C) MAD
   - (D) BLACK

9. SAME
   - (A) SHY
   - (B) SHAME
   - (C) OPPOSITE
   - (D) ALIKE

OLYMPIAD WORKBOOK (IEO) CLASS – 1

10. BIG
    (A) LARGE
    (B) PLENTY
    (C) EMPTY
    (D) ELEPHANT
11. QUIET
    (A) LEAVE
    (B) GLOOMY
    (C) SILENT
    (D) QUIT
12. JUMP
    (A) LEAP   (B) FLY
    (C) CROSS   (D) ROPE

13. START
    (A) BEGIN
    (B) STOP
    (C) END
    (D) PLAY
14. FAST
    (A) SLOW
    (B) SPEED
    (C) QUICK
    (D) HUNGRY
15. NEAR
    (A) FAR   (B) DEAR
    (C) UP   (D) CLOSE

HOTS (ACHIEVERS SECTION)

Circle the meaning of the underlined word from the given options.

For example:

The artist sat down to <u>draw</u>.
    (A) play
    (B) mould
    (C) sketch
    (D) take

16. Please <u>shut</u> the door.
    (A) silent   (B) close
    (C) bang   (D) pull
17. The soil is <u>wet</u> due to the rain.
    (A) damp   (B) loose
    (C) dry   (D) rain

18. His father is a very <u>rich</u> man.
    (A) strong
    (B) money
    (C) poor
    (D) wealthy
19. The guests <u>came</u> late.
    (A) ate   (B) go
    (C) became   (D) arrived
20. I am <u>afraid</u> of dark.
    (A) lost   (B) light
    (C) scared   (D) heavy

Darken Your Choice with HB Pencil

1.	Ⓐ Ⓑ Ⓒ Ⓓ	5.	Ⓐ Ⓑ Ⓒ Ⓓ	9.	Ⓐ Ⓑ Ⓒ Ⓓ	13	Ⓐ Ⓑ Ⓒ Ⓓ	17.	Ⓐ Ⓑ Ⓒ Ⓓ
2.	Ⓐ Ⓑ Ⓒ Ⓓ	6.	Ⓐ Ⓑ Ⓒ Ⓓ	10.	Ⓐ Ⓑ Ⓒ Ⓓ	14.	Ⓐ Ⓑ Ⓒ Ⓓ	18.	Ⓐ Ⓑ Ⓒ Ⓓ
3.	Ⓐ Ⓑ Ⓒ Ⓓ	7.	Ⓐ Ⓑ Ⓒ Ⓓ	11.	Ⓐ Ⓑ Ⓒ Ⓓ	15.	Ⓐ Ⓑ Ⓒ Ⓓ	19.	Ⓐ Ⓑ Ⓒ Ⓓ
4.	Ⓐ Ⓑ Ⓒ Ⓓ	8.	Ⓐ Ⓑ Ⓒ Ⓓ	12.	Ⓐ Ⓑ Ⓒ Ⓓ	16.	Ⓐ Ⓑ Ⓒ Ⓓ	20.	Ⓐ Ⓑ Ⓒ Ⓓ

WORDS AND THEIR OPPOSITES

LEARNING OBJECTIVES

➤ Different words and their opposite words

PRACTICE EXERCISE

Match the following words with their opposites. The first two have been done for you.

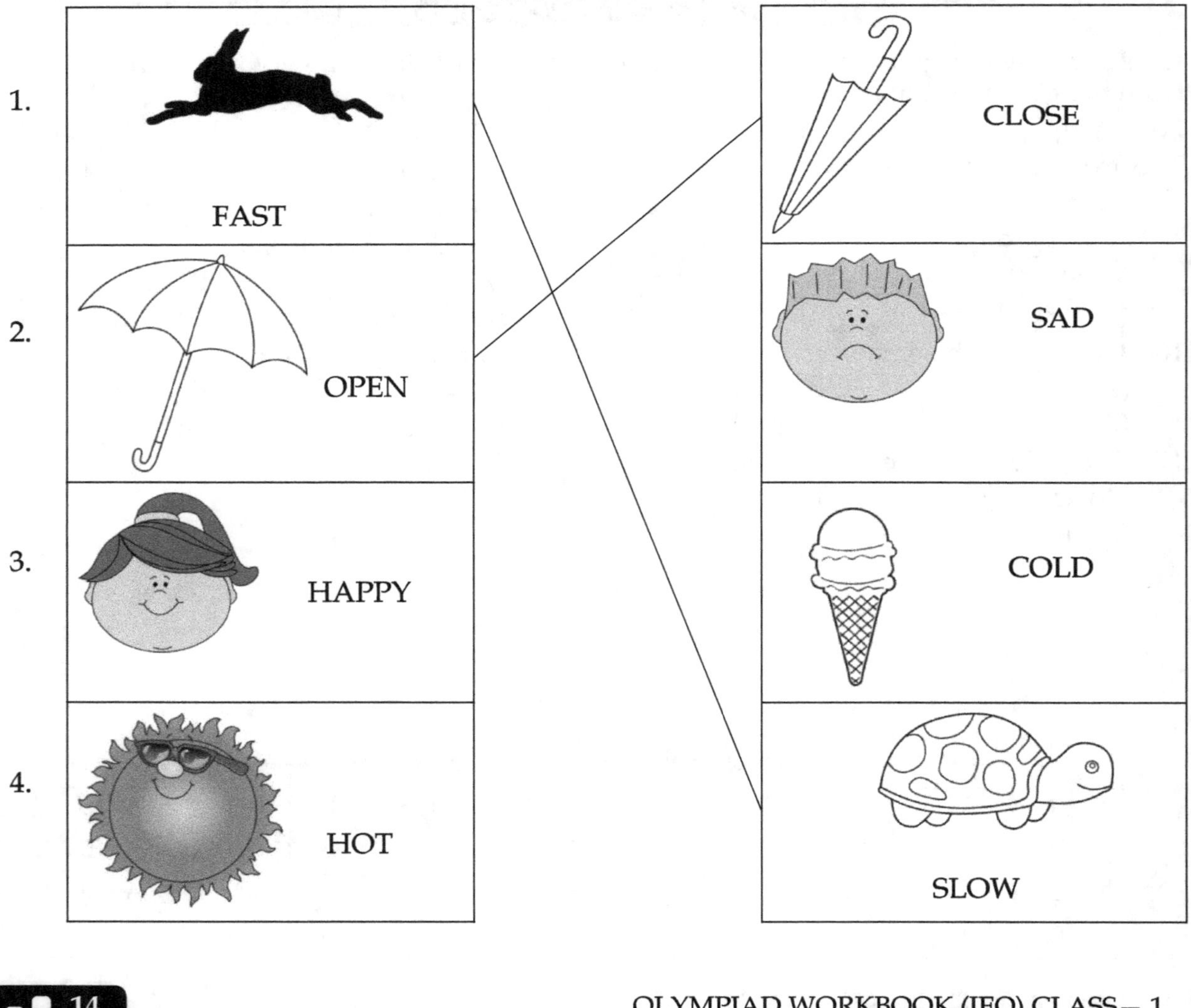

1.	FAST	CLOSE
2.	OPEN	SAD
3.	HAPPY	COLD
4.	HOT	SLOW

OLYMPIAD WORKBOOK (IEO) CLASS— 1

5. OLD
6. BITTER
7. HARD
8. HEALTHY
9. HEAVY
10. INSIDE
11. NOISY
12. SHARP

SWEET
YOUNG
LIGHT
SILENT
OUTSIDE
BLUNT
SOFT
UNHEALTHY

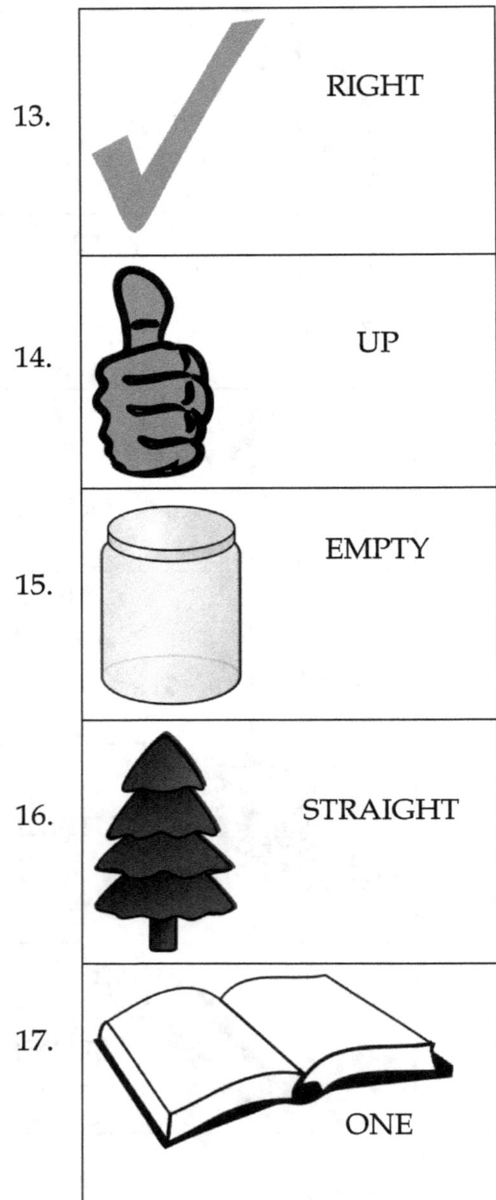

13.   RIGHT   DOWN

14.   UP   BENT

15.   EMPTY   MANY

16.   STRAIGHT   WRONG

17.   ONE   FULL

Write the opposite of the following words. The first one has been done for you.

S. No.	Word	Opposite
18.	Give	Take
19.	Hairy	
20.	Bright	
21.	Absent	
22.	Before	

1.	Ⓐ Ⓑ Ⓒ Ⓓ	6.	Ⓐ Ⓑ Ⓒ Ⓓ	11.	Ⓐ Ⓑ Ⓒ Ⓓ	16	Ⓐ Ⓑ Ⓒ Ⓓ	21.	Ⓐ Ⓑ Ⓒ Ⓓ
2.	Ⓐ Ⓑ Ⓒ Ⓓ	7.	Ⓐ Ⓑ Ⓒ Ⓓ	12.	Ⓐ Ⓑ Ⓒ Ⓓ	17.	Ⓐ Ⓑ Ⓒ Ⓓ	22.	Ⓐ Ⓑ Ⓒ Ⓓ
3.	Ⓐ Ⓑ Ⓒ Ⓓ	8.	Ⓐ Ⓑ Ⓒ Ⓓ	13.	Ⓐ Ⓑ Ⓒ Ⓓ	18.	Ⓐ Ⓑ Ⓒ Ⓓ		
4.	Ⓐ Ⓑ Ⓒ Ⓓ	9.	Ⓐ Ⓑ Ⓒ Ⓓ	14.	Ⓐ Ⓑ Ⓒ Ⓓ	19.	Ⓐ Ⓑ Ⓒ Ⓓ		
5.	Ⓐ Ⓑ Ⓒ Ⓓ	10.	Ⓐ Ⓑ Ⓒ Ⓓ	15.	Ⓐ Ⓑ Ⓒ Ⓓ	20.	Ⓐ Ⓑ Ⓒ Ⓓ		

FEMININE AND MASCULINE (GENDER)

LEARNING OBJECTIVES

➤ Feminine and Masculine concepts

PRACTICE EXERCISE

Write 'Masculine' or 'Feminine' against each word. The first two have been done for you.

S. No.	Words	Masculine/Feminine
1.	Father	Masculine
2.	Sister	Feminine
3.	Gentleman	

4.		
5.		
6.		
7.		

8.	Princess	
9.	Bride	
10.	Mare	
11.	Lion	

12.	 Peacock	
13.	 Tigress	
14.	 Wizard	

15.	 Mr. Smith	
16.	 Miss Jones	
17.	 Duck	

Write the feminine gender of the following. The first two have been done for you.

18. Grandfather	Grandmother
19. Policeman	Policewoman
20. Washerman	
21. Prince	
22. Lion	

1. Ⓐ Ⓑ Ⓒ Ⓓ	6. Ⓐ Ⓑ Ⓒ Ⓓ	11. Ⓐ Ⓑ Ⓒ Ⓓ	16 Ⓐ Ⓑ Ⓒ Ⓓ	21. Ⓐ Ⓑ Ⓒ Ⓓ
2. Ⓐ Ⓑ Ⓒ Ⓓ	7. Ⓐ Ⓑ Ⓒ Ⓓ	12. Ⓐ Ⓑ Ⓒ Ⓓ	17. Ⓐ Ⓑ Ⓒ Ⓓ	22. Ⓐ Ⓑ Ⓒ Ⓓ
3. Ⓐ Ⓑ Ⓒ Ⓓ	8. Ⓐ Ⓑ Ⓒ Ⓓ	13. Ⓐ Ⓑ Ⓒ Ⓓ	18. Ⓐ Ⓑ Ⓒ Ⓓ	
4. Ⓐ Ⓑ Ⓒ Ⓓ	9. Ⓐ Ⓑ Ⓒ Ⓓ	14. Ⓐ Ⓑ Ⓒ Ⓓ	19. Ⓐ Ⓑ Ⓒ Ⓓ	
5. Ⓐ Ⓑ Ⓒ Ⓓ	10. Ⓐ Ⓑ Ⓒ Ⓓ	15. Ⓐ Ⓑ Ⓒ Ⓓ	20. Ⓐ Ⓑ Ⓒ Ⓓ	

WORD PAIRS AND ODD ONE OUT

PRACTICE EXERCISE

Using the pictures as clues, write the correct pair word for the given words.

S. No.	Word	Picture
1.	KNIFE	
2.	APPLES	
3.	FLOWER	

OLYMPIAD WORKBOOK (IEO) CLASS – 1

4.	BOW	
5.	NEEDLE	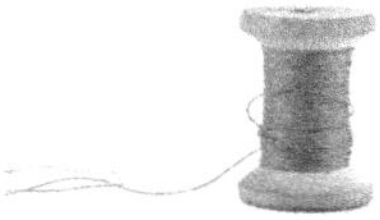
6.	BIRDS	
7.	BAT	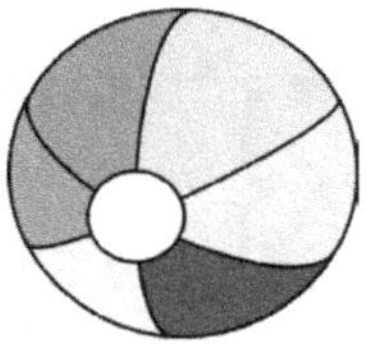
8.	POTS	
9.	SHOES	
10.	HAMMER	

11.	SUN	
12.	LOCK	
13.	HUSBAND	
14.	PEN	
15.	BOY	

Find the odd one out. The first one has been done for you.

16. (A) LION   (B) COW
   (C) GOAT   (D) BUFFALO

17. (A) RED   (B) RAINBOW
   (C) YELLOW   (D) BLUE

18. (A) FISH   (B) BIRD
   (C) OCTOPUS   (D) SHARK

19. (A) EARRINGS   (B) NECKLACE
   (C) SHIRT   (D) BANGLE

20. (A) LIPS   (B) EYES
   (C) EARS   (D) NOSE RING

21. (A) BRINJAL   (B) APPLE
   (C) ORANGE   (D) GRAPES

22. (A) SOFA   (B) COMPUTER
   (C) CHAIR   (D) TABLE

23. (A) TRUCK   (B) BICYCLE
  (C) HORSE   (D) CAR
24. (A) LAMP   (B) FAN
  (C) BOOK   (D) TELEVISION

25. (A) CABBAGE (B) ROSE
  (C) LOTUS   (D) JASMINE

HOTS (ACHIEVERS SECTION)

Complete the word pairs.

26. I would like some salt and _____________ on my salad.
27. Mary had bread and _____________ for breakfast.
28. It rained cats and _____________ yesterday.

Find the odd one out.

29. (A) NOSE   (B) LIPS
  (C) TEETH   (D) TONGUE
30. (A) THUMB   (B) TOES
  (C) FINGERS (D) WRIST

1.	Ⓐ Ⓑ Ⓒ Ⓓ	7.	Ⓐ Ⓑ Ⓒ Ⓓ	13.	Ⓐ Ⓑ Ⓒ Ⓓ	19	Ⓐ Ⓑ Ⓒ Ⓓ	25.	Ⓐ Ⓑ Ⓒ Ⓓ
2.	Ⓐ Ⓑ Ⓒ Ⓓ	8.	Ⓐ Ⓑ Ⓒ Ⓓ	14.	Ⓐ Ⓑ Ⓒ Ⓓ	20.	Ⓐ Ⓑ Ⓒ Ⓓ	26.	Ⓐ Ⓑ Ⓒ Ⓓ
3.	Ⓐ Ⓑ Ⓒ Ⓓ	9.	Ⓐ Ⓑ Ⓒ Ⓓ	15.	Ⓐ Ⓑ Ⓒ Ⓓ	21.	Ⓐ Ⓑ Ⓒ Ⓓ	27.	Ⓐ Ⓑ Ⓒ Ⓓ
4.	Ⓐ Ⓑ Ⓒ Ⓓ	10.	Ⓐ Ⓑ Ⓒ Ⓓ	16.	Ⓐ Ⓑ Ⓒ Ⓓ	22.	Ⓐ Ⓑ Ⓒ Ⓓ	28.	Ⓐ Ⓑ Ⓒ Ⓓ
5.	Ⓐ Ⓑ Ⓒ Ⓓ	11.	Ⓐ Ⓑ Ⓒ Ⓓ	17.	Ⓐ Ⓑ Ⓒ Ⓓ	23.	Ⓐ Ⓑ Ⓒ Ⓓ	29.	Ⓐ Ⓑ Ⓒ Ⓓ
6.	Ⓐ Ⓑ Ⓒ Ⓓ	12.	Ⓐ Ⓑ Ⓒ Ⓓ	18.	Ⓐ Ⓑ Ⓒ Ⓓ	24.	Ⓐ Ⓑ Ⓒ Ⓓ	30.	Ⓐ Ⓑ Ⓒ Ⓓ

ANIMALS AND THEIR YOUNG ONES

6

LEARNING OBJECTIVES

➤ Different animals and their young ones

PRACTICE EXERCISE

Write the names of the young ones of the following:

S. No.	Animal	Young One
1.	Bird	
2.	Eagle	
3.	Fish	
4.	Fox	
5.	Frog	
6.	Goose	
7.	Swan	
8.	Owl	
9.	Panda	
10.	Rat	
11.	Seal	
12.	Whale	
13.	Turkey	
14.	Zebra	
15.	Rabbit	

OLYMPIAD WORKBOOK (IEO) CLASS – 1

Look at the images of the animals below and write the name of their young ones.

16. The young one of a HEN is called _______________________.

17. The young one of a SHEEP is called _______________________.

18. The young one of a HORSE is called _______________________.

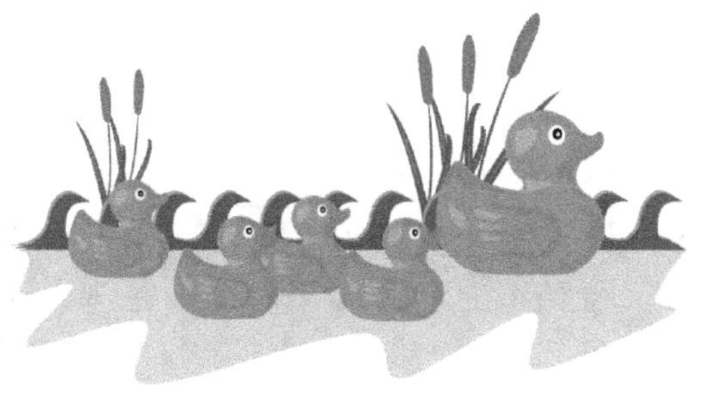

19. The young one of a DUCK is called _______________________.

20. The young one of a DEER is called _______________________.

---Darken Your Choice with HB Pencil---

1.	A B C D	5.	A B C D	9.	A B C D	13	A B C D	17.	A B C D
2.	A B C D	6.	A B C D	10.	A B C D	14.	A B C D	18.	A B C D
3.	A B C D	7.	A B C D	11.	A B C D	15.	A B C D	19.	A B C D
4.	A B C D	8.	A B C D	12.	A B C D	16.	A B C D	20.	A B C D

NOUNS

LEARNING OBJECTIVES

➤ Usage of Noun

PRACTICE EXERCISE

Write against each whether it is the name of a person, place, animal or thing.

1.	JAPAN	
2.	BUTTER	
3.	MR. RICH	
4.	DRIVER	
5.	ZEBRA	
6.	SCHOOL	
7.	PARK	
8.	MAN	
9.	CRAYONS	
10.	ELEPHANT	
11.	OCTOPUS	
12.	COMPUTER	
13.	MARKET	
14.	AUNT	
15.	EAGLE	

Direction 16-18: Fill in the blanks with appropriate noun.

16. When I was a young child I liked to watch a _____ of cattle grazing on grasses.

17. Bird flu can kill a large _______ of chickens in two days.

18. This _______ of black ants ate my bread and chicken last night.

Directions: 19–20. Form abstract nouns for the following.

19. Long: _______________

20. Strong: _______________

HOTS (ACHIEVERS SECTION)

Identify and underline the nouns in the following sentences. The first two have been done for you.

21. The little <u>boy</u> helped the blind <u>man</u> cross the <u>road</u>.

22. A beautiful <u>bird</u> has built a <u>nest</u> outside my <u>house</u>.

23. The teacher scolded me for being late to school.

24. The robbers stole all the money and jewellery in the safe.

25. Malaria is caused by a mosquito bite.

PRONOUN

LEARNING OBJECTIVES

➤ Pronouns and its usage

PRACTICE EXERCISE

I. Fill in the blanks with correct option:

1. Ashoka was a great warrior. _______ won many wars.
   (A) They
   (B) She
   (C) He
   (D) It

2. Children are very happy because _____ are going on a trip.
   (A) He
   (B) They
   (C) She
   (D) It

3. Angelina is a pretty girl. _______ studies in class 1.
   (A) She
   (B) He
   (C) They
   (D) It

4. I like this book. ______ has many pictures.
   (A) He
   (B) You
   (C) I
   (D) It

5. _______ am going to learn French.
   (A) They
   (B) I
   (C) He
   (D) She

II. Use the correct pronoun for the following sentences using the bracket options

6. The chair is brown. (It/He)

7. My mother is a teacher. (She/He)

8. The bell is ringing. (It/They)

9. The three boys are flying kites. (They/It)

10. The mobile is ringing. (It/They)

11. Mohan and I are going to a birthday party. (They/We)

12. Sarla likes to dance. (He/She)

13. The lion is the king of the jungle. (He/It)

14. The gentleman is my neighbour. (He/She)

15. The dog was happy when we played with _________ (It/She/He)

Identify the pronoun in the following sentences.

16. James is an honest boy. He never tells a lie.
    (A) An   (B) James
    (C) He   (D) Lie

17. She wants to win the competition.
    (A) She   (B) To
    (C) Win   (D) The

18. They want to go for a long walk.
    (A) Want   (B) Go
    (C) For   (D) They

19. Where is your car? Is it in the garage?
    (A) Is   (B) It
    (C) Where   (D) The

20. I don't want to work anymore.
    (A) To   (B) Work
    (C) Anymore   (D) I

—————————Darken Your Choice with HB Pencil —————————

1.	Ⓐ Ⓑ Ⓒ Ⓓ	5.	Ⓐ Ⓑ Ⓒ Ⓓ	9.	Ⓐ Ⓑ Ⓒ Ⓓ	13	Ⓐ Ⓑ Ⓒ Ⓓ	17.	Ⓐ Ⓑ Ⓒ Ⓓ
2.	Ⓐ Ⓑ Ⓒ Ⓓ	6.	Ⓐ Ⓑ Ⓒ Ⓓ	10.	Ⓐ Ⓑ Ⓒ Ⓓ	14.	Ⓐ Ⓑ Ⓒ Ⓓ	18.	Ⓐ Ⓑ Ⓒ Ⓓ
3.	Ⓐ Ⓑ Ⓒ Ⓓ	7.	Ⓐ Ⓑ Ⓒ Ⓓ	11.	Ⓐ Ⓑ Ⓒ Ⓓ	15.	Ⓐ Ⓑ Ⓒ Ⓓ	19.	Ⓐ Ⓑ Ⓒ Ⓓ
4.	Ⓐ Ⓑ Ⓒ Ⓓ	8.	Ⓐ Ⓑ Ⓒ Ⓓ	12.	Ⓐ Ⓑ Ⓒ Ⓓ	16.	Ⓐ Ⓑ Ⓒ Ⓓ	20.	Ⓐ Ⓑ Ⓒ Ⓓ

VERBS

LEARNING OBJECTIVES

➤ Basic concept of Verbs

PRACTICE EXERCISE

Underline the verb/verbs in the following sentences. The first one has been done for you.

1. Jack and Jill <u>went</u> up the hill.
2. The clock struck 12 at midnight.
3. The painting fell down and broke.
4. Humpty Dumpty sat on a wall.
5. The mouse ran up the clock.
6. Incy Wincy spider climbed up the water spout.
7. She sang and her brother played the guitar around the campfire.
8. My mother likes tea, and my father likes coffee.
9. He helped his mother clean the house.
10. Mother usually wraps all the gifts on Christmas eve.
11. Jack threw the beans away.
12. Birds and forest animals helped Snow White clean the house.
13. The football fans sat in front of the television.
14. I brush my teeth, take a bath, and eat my breakfast evening morning.
15. She reads books for pleasure.
16. Please bring me some coffee.

HOTS (ACHIEVERS SECTION)

Find the verb/verbs from the following options. The first two have been done for you.

17. (A) SEE   (B) THEATRE
    (C) ACT   (D) ACTORS
18. (A) SHARP   (B) FRUITS
    (C) DRIVE   (D) CUT
19. (A) SPORTS   (B) PLAY
    (C) WASH   (D) CRICKET
20. (A) OLD   (B) KILL
    (C) FIND   (D) GREAT
21. (A) PAINT   (B) REPAIR
    (C) DECEMBER   (D) SONG
22. (A) NEW   (B) GREEN
    (C) COOK   (D) SING
23. (A) OCEAN   (B) SWIM
    (C) RIVER   (D) LAKE

24. (A) CHOP   (B) DRINK | 25. (A) FOOTBALL (B) KICK
    (C) PEN   (D) LETTER | (C) CATCH   (D) TENNIS

ARTICLES 

LEARNING OBJECTIVES

➤ Usage of Articles

PRACTICE EXERCISE

Fill in the blanks with 'a' or 'an'. The first two have been done for you.

1. Billy celebrated his birthday at <u>an</u> orphanage.
2. I bought <u>a</u> red car.
3. I saw _____ football match yesterday.
4. He climbed onto the bed on seeing _____ cockroach.
5. The farmer had _____ cow and _____ ox.
6. Will you tell me _____ story?
7. Harry Potter had _____ owl and Hermione had _____ cat.
8. I ate _____ egg sandwich and _____ pie for lunch.
9. _____ mouse lives in the tree in front of my house.
10. Mary had _____ little lamb.
11. My aunt gifted me _____ ink pen and _____ box of chocolates.
12. _____ artist uses _____ easel to paint.
13. There is _____ story about _____ lion and _____ rabbit in my book.
14. When I grow up, I want to be _____ engineer.
15. I have _____ uncle and _____ aunt who live in England.
16. The doctor gave me _____ tablet that made the fever go away.
17. My school is _____ mile away from my house.

HOTS (ACHIEVERS SECTION)

Write 'a' or 'an' in the blanks. The first two have been done for you.

18. <u>A</u> bright, sunny day
19. <u>An</u> interesting story
20. _____ apple pie
21. _____ red crayon
22. _____ roasted chicken
23. _____ almond cake
24. _____ colourful clown
25. _____ university
26. _____ orange raincoat
27. _____ indoor plant
28. _____ western country
29. _____ English pie

30. _______ German soldier

31. _______ oil painting

32. _______ horror movie

33. _______ acting course

34. _______ award ceremony

PREPOSITIONS

LEARNING OBJECTIVES

➤ Concept of Prepositions

PRACTICE EXERCISE

Fill in the blanks with the most suitable option.

1. The kids were playing _______ the street.
   (A) on
   (B) under
   (C) in
   (D) with

2. There were many people ____________ the concert.
   (A) at
   (B) on
   (C) behind
   (D) with

3. The sun disappeared ____________ the clouds.
   (A) at
   (B) behind
   (C) with
   (D) on

4. There is a mark ____________ your shirt.
   (A) under
   (B) in
   (C) on
   (D) at

5. Have you looked ____________ the bed?
   (A) at
   (B) in
   (C) about
   (D) under

6. I have a client ____________ me right now.
   (A) with
   (B) in
   (C) behind
   (D) on

7. He was lying ____________ the floor.
   (A) under
   (B) on
   (C) with
   (D) in

8. I will meet you ____________ the main entrance.
   (A) on
   (B) in
   (C) at
   (D) with

9. She is waiting for you ____________ the sitting room.
   (A) below
   (B) under
   (C) on
   (D) in

10. We took shelter under an oak tree.
    (A) under
    (B) on
    (C) at
    (D) in

Fill in the blanks with the most suitable option.

11. The boy is going _________ the fence. (through, under)

12. The girl is coming _________ the stairs. (around, down)

13. The children are swimming _________ the river. (under, across)

14. The teacher is standing _________ the student. (towards, between)

15. The parrot is sitting _________ the branch. (on, between)

ADJECTIVES

LEARNING OBJECTIVES

➤ Basics of Adjectives

PRACTICE EXERCISE

Identify the adjectives in the following sentences.

1. The mangoes are ripe.
   - (A) The
   - (B) Mangoes
   - (C) Are
   - (D) Ripe

2. Our cat has small ears.
   - (A) Cat
   - (B) Small
   - (C) Ears
   - (D) Has

3. Bolt is a fast runner.
   - (A) Fast
   - (B) Runner
   - (C) Bolt
   - (D) A

4. There is a round table in my room.
   - (A) room
   - (B) there
   - (C) round
   - (D) table

5. There were many flowers in the shop but I liked the red one.
   - (A) One
   - (B) Red
   - (C) Were
   - (D) Flowers

6. A spider has eight legs.
   - (A) Legs
   - (B) Spider
   - (C) Has
   - (D) Eight

7. The cat with a long tail ran after a mouse.
   - (A) The
   - (B) Tail
   - (C) Long
   - (D) Ran

8. An old man is waiting for you outside the school.
   - (A) Old
   - (B) Waiting
   - (C) You
   - (D) School

9. A giraffe has a long neck.
   - (A) Giraffe
   - (B) Neck
   - (C) A
   - (D) Long

10. I saw a huge elephant in the zoo.
    - (A) Saw
    - (B) Huge
    - (C) Zoo
    - (D) Elephant

Fill in the blanks with suitable adjectives from brackets.

11. The packet is very ____________ (heavy/young).

12. Delhi is a __________ city. (round/big).

13. Respecting elders is a ____________ habit. (good/bad).

14. When it rains, the road gets __________ (dry/muddy).

COMPREHENSION

PRACTICE EXERCISE

1. How many balls did the dog find?
2. What colour was the ball that the dog played with?
3. What did the dog do with the yellow ball?
4. What did the dog do with the blue ball?
5. What did the dog do with the red ball?
6. List pairs of rhyming words from the poem.

   _______________________ and _______________________

   _______________________ and _______________________

   _______________________ and _______________________

   _______________________ and _______________________

7. What is a bee's home called?

   ____

8. Who is this?
   (A) Beth   (B) Kim   (C) Jim   (D) Rob

9. Who is this?
   (A) Beth   (B) Kim   (C) Jim   (D) Rob

10. Who is the singer?

____

11. What does Beth play?

____

12. Write down the names of all the members of the rock band.

(A) _____________________________   (B) _____________________________

(C) _____________________________   (D) _____________________________

(E) _____________________________

13. What is Beth's problem?

____

14. How was her problem solved?

____

1.	Ⓐ Ⓑ Ⓒ Ⓓ	4.	Ⓐ Ⓑ Ⓒ Ⓓ	7.	Ⓐ Ⓑ Ⓒ Ⓓ	10.	Ⓐ Ⓑ Ⓒ Ⓓ	13.	Ⓐ Ⓑ Ⓒ Ⓓ
2.	Ⓐ Ⓑ Ⓒ Ⓓ	5.	Ⓐ Ⓑ Ⓒ Ⓓ	8.	Ⓐ Ⓑ Ⓒ Ⓓ	11.	Ⓐ Ⓑ Ⓒ Ⓓ	14.	Ⓐ Ⓑ Ⓒ Ⓓ
3.	Ⓐ Ⓑ Ⓒ Ⓓ	6.	Ⓐ Ⓑ Ⓒ Ⓓ	9.	Ⓐ Ⓑ Ⓒ Ⓓ	12.	Ⓐ Ⓑ Ⓒ Ⓓ		

SPOKEN AND WRITTEN EXPRESSION; PUNCTUATION

LEARNING OBJECTIVES

➤ Spoken Expressions
➤ Written expression

PRACTICE EXERCISE

Directions: Read the sentences carefully and answer them from the options given below

1. I am not going there.
   (A) Sure thanks
   (B) No, thanks
   (C) Why? Are you not well?
   (D) Thanks

2. Alok: Do you like eating pizza?
   Ansh: ______________.
   (A) How do I know?
   (B) They are going.
   (C) That's ok
   (D) Yes, I like eating pizza.

3. Adil: is he your brother?
   Sameer: __________.
   (A) He is ok
   (B) He is going
   (C) No, he is my neighbour
   (D) I am good

4. Aman: hello! How are you?
   Koran: __________.
   (A) I am fine. How about you?
   (B) See you tomorrow
   (C) Nothing much
   (D) No, I am eating food.

5. Ankit: Thanks for coming for the party
   Golu:
   (A) Oh, don't mind
   (B) My pleasure
   (C) You are always welcome
   (D) That's ok

6. Mom: Ram you go and play
   Ram: ________
   (A) He is painting a picture
   (B) He is riding a horse
   (C) Ok, Mom.
   (D) I am eating.

7. Hello: can I talk to Geeta?
   (A) Hello, are you talking to Seema?
   (B) Hello, can you speak with Reema?
   (C) Yes, may I know who is speaking?
   (D) Seema is not there

8. Hello, I am Karen
   (A) He is not coming
   (B) They are friends
   (C) I am 8 years old
   (D) He is playing right now.

9. Mr. Smith: I have lost my dog
    Mr. Caren: ______________
    (A) His dog loves bones
    (B) I have lost my bat
    (C) Oh! Did you report to the police?
    (D) I am going
10. This is my book.
    (A) He is driving his car
    (B) Ok. You can take it.
    (C) He is my cousin
    (D) I ate my food on time
11. I hurt my toe
    (A) Sure, I will try
    (B) Oh! Did you take some medicine?
    (C) Thanks its ok
    (D) My pleasure
12. Rekha Went to the garden today
    (A) She will get sand
    (B) She will pick flowers
    (C) She will eat food
    (D) She will play with her friends.
13. Sarah: I love Going to beach Sharon: ______
    (A) It was good
    (B) Sure, thanks
    (C) Even I like going there
    (D) He is studying
14. Anuj: Mom I am going out to play.
    Mom; ________
    (A) Ok, but come back before its dark.
    (B) He is reading a book
    (C) He has to go somewhere
    (D) I am busy. I can't come

15. I have fever, ______.
    (A) Don't worry,
    (B) Sure, thanks
    (C) I will visit doctor
    (D) He is watching TV
16. Did you study for the exam today?
    (A) Its ok.
    (B) Thanks. I want to go
    (C) Yes, I did.
    (D) No, let him take it.
17. Boss: Will you please finish your work?
    Sam: ________
    (A) Thanks, but I don't eat burgers
    (B) Sure. Sir! Don't worry.
    (C) This is my car
    (D) Today is my birthday
18. Whom are you waiting for?
    (A) I am waiting for my dad.
    (B) No. I am going
    (C) Its my birthday today
    (D) Yes I am waiting.
19. Its my birthday today
    (A) Sure, I'll come
    (B) Happy birthday to you!
    (C) He will not go
    (D) This is my house
20. Do you want to watch a movie?
    (A) I don't like watching movies
    (B) See you tomorrow
    (C) Give me some food to eat
    (D) He has already gone.

HOTS (ACHIEVERS SECTION)

Read the passage carefully and answer the following questions

Ram was a very good boy. He was very good instudies. Ram always said"________"(21). But his mom always told him to be very careful. She said________ (22). One day he had a test in English. When he saw the paper he was very excited. Hesaid ________. (23). He hoped to get full marks. But his class teacher told him to be very careful. But Ram was confident. He said that ________ (24). On the other hand, his friend Amar was silent. He told Ram to keep quiet too. To which Ram said______ (25). Ram was the first one to finish the paper. But ________ (26). He got only 22 out of 30. Ram had forgotten to answer many questions. He got sad. Amar got full marks. He did his work carefully. His teacher called him and told him"________"(27). Always recheck________ (28). Sunil Promised ________ (29). And Said"__________"(30)

21.
 (A) That I cannot be wrong,
 (B) That I am going.
 (C) Eat green vegetables
 (D) This is my house

22.
 (A) Always be careful
 (B) Go to school
 (C) Do not play
 (D) do not study

23.
 (A) The test is very easy
 (B) That I am eating food.
 (C) sure, thanks
 (D) This is my bicycle

24.
 (A) I will fail
 (B) I want to play
 (C) This is my house
 (D) I will get full marks.

25.
 (A) He is going
 (B) He is my cousin
 (C) May be he does not know the paper,
 (D) I am Five years old.

26.
 (A) When the result came
 (B) When he went out
 (C) He started searching
 (D) Its morning right now.

27.
 (A) I will eat good food
 (B) Be careful next time
 (C) Do not give papers
 (D) Give back my book to me.

28.
 (A) Then go out
 (B) Then answer
 (C) Then eat
 (D) I Want to play

29.
 (A) To go out.
 (B) To never eat pizza (Value Based)
 (C) To be careful next time.
 (D) I will kneel before you

30.
 (A) Ma'am I will be careful in future
 (B) Sure, thanks
 (C) Sorry, I am late
 (D) I missed my bus

	A B C D		A B C D		A B C D		A B C D		A B C D
1.	Ⓐ Ⓑ Ⓒ Ⓓ	7.	Ⓐ Ⓑ Ⓒ Ⓓ	13.	Ⓐ Ⓑ Ⓒ Ⓓ	19	Ⓐ Ⓑ Ⓒ Ⓓ	25.	Ⓐ Ⓑ Ⓒ Ⓓ
2.	Ⓐ Ⓑ Ⓒ Ⓓ	8.	Ⓐ Ⓑ Ⓒ Ⓓ	14.	Ⓐ Ⓑ Ⓒ Ⓓ	20.	Ⓐ Ⓑ Ⓒ Ⓓ	26.	Ⓐ Ⓑ Ⓒ Ⓓ
3.	Ⓐ Ⓑ Ⓒ Ⓓ	9.	Ⓐ Ⓑ Ⓒ Ⓓ	15.	Ⓐ Ⓑ Ⓒ Ⓓ	21.	Ⓐ Ⓑ Ⓒ Ⓓ	27.	Ⓐ Ⓑ Ⓒ Ⓓ
4.	Ⓐ Ⓑ Ⓒ Ⓓ	10.	Ⓐ Ⓑ Ⓒ Ⓓ	16.	Ⓐ Ⓑ Ⓒ Ⓓ	22.	Ⓐ Ⓑ Ⓒ Ⓓ	28.	Ⓐ Ⓑ Ⓒ Ⓓ
5.	Ⓐ Ⓑ Ⓒ Ⓓ	11.	Ⓐ Ⓑ Ⓒ Ⓓ	17.	Ⓐ Ⓑ Ⓒ Ⓓ	23.	Ⓐ Ⓑ Ⓒ Ⓓ	29.	Ⓐ Ⓑ Ⓒ Ⓓ
6.	Ⓐ Ⓑ Ⓒ Ⓓ	12.	Ⓐ Ⓑ Ⓒ Ⓓ	18.	Ⓐ Ⓑ Ⓒ Ⓓ	24.	Ⓐ Ⓑ Ⓒ Ⓓ	30.	Ⓐ Ⓑ Ⓒ Ⓓ

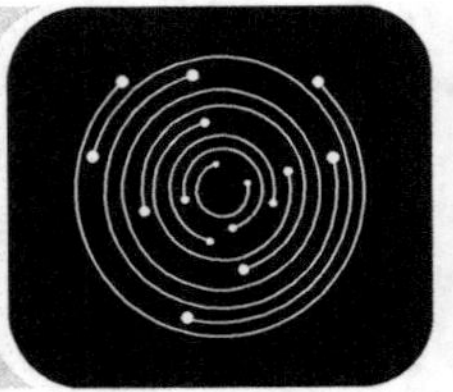

MODEL TEST PAPER

WORD AND STRUCTURE KNOWLEDGE

1. Find the odd one out.
   (A) RED (B) YELLOW
   (C) COLOUR (D) BLACK

2. Identify the picture and choose the correct option.

   (A) CHIPS
   (B) WATERMELON
   (C) TENT
   (D) BOAT

Direction (Q. No. 3 and 4): Fill in the blanks with the suitable word pairs.

3. A bat hangs upside ___________ to take a nap.
   (A) BACK (B) FRONT
   (C) DOWN (D) LEFT

4. The boys played catch and _________ with the ball.
   (A) PULL (B) HATCH
   (C) THROW (D) CATCH

Direction (Q. No. 5 and 6): Form a meaningful word.

5. NEAOC
   (A) OCEAN (B) ANEOC
   (C) NOCEA (D) EACON

6. NDOUS
   (A) OUNDS (B) SOUND
   (C) UNODS (D) DOUNS

7. Write the feminine noun of the following:
   Masculine   Feminine
   Man

8. 'The clown balanced himself on a ball'. Identify the noun/nouns.
   (A) Balanced
   (B) Clown
   (C) Ball
   (D) Both (B) and (C)

9. Write the opposite of the following:
   Sink   X   _________________

READING

Direction (Q. No. 10 to 13): Look at the picture given below and answer the questions that follow.

10. I am a _________.
    (A) Sheep   (B) Cow
    (C) Goat   (D) Pig
11. A male pig is called a boar. The feminine noun of boar is _________.
    (A) Sow
    (B) Cow
    (C) Ewe
    (D) Mare
12. The nose of a pig is called ______________.
    (A) Nostril
    (B) Beak
    (C) Snout
    (D) Feather
13. My young one is called a ______________.
    (A) Calf
    (B) Piglet
    (C) Fawn
    (D) Foal

SPOKEN AND WRITTEN EXPRESSION

Direction (Q. No. 14 and 15): Choose the correct answer.

14. Teacher: 'Who spilled glue on the desk?'.
    John: ______________________
    (A) Sorry teacher, I did.
    (B) How dare you ask me this question?
    (C) Is there more glue?
    (D) Ask someone else.
15. Mother set a pot of soup to boil.
    ____
    (A) The bread was very hard.
    (B) The smell of the soup made us all very hungry.
    (C) There were no vegetables in the house.
    (D) I am not going to the market.

—Darken Your Choice with HB Pencil—

1. Ⓐ Ⓑ Ⓒ Ⓓ	4. Ⓐ Ⓑ Ⓒ Ⓓ	7. Ⓐ Ⓑ Ⓒ Ⓓ	10. Ⓐ Ⓑ Ⓒ Ⓓ	13. Ⓐ Ⓑ Ⓒ Ⓓ
2. Ⓐ Ⓑ Ⓒ Ⓓ	5. Ⓐ Ⓑ Ⓒ Ⓓ	8. Ⓐ Ⓑ Ⓒ Ⓓ	11. Ⓐ Ⓑ Ⓒ Ⓓ	14. Ⓐ Ⓑ Ⓒ Ⓓ
3. Ⓐ Ⓑ Ⓒ Ⓓ	6. Ⓐ Ⓑ Ⓒ Ⓓ	9. Ⓐ Ⓑ Ⓒ Ⓓ	12. Ⓐ Ⓑ Ⓒ Ⓓ	15. Ⓐ Ⓑ Ⓒ Ⓓ

HINTS AND SOLUTIONS

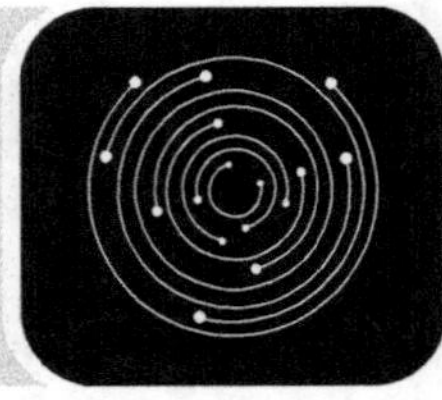

1. JUMBLED WORDS; IDENTIFYING A WORD FROM THE PICTURE

Answer Key

1. (B)	2. (C)	3. (D)	4. (A)	5. (D)	6. (C)	7. (A)	8. (C)	9. (C)	10 (D)
11. (A)	12. (B)	13. (D)	14. (A)	15. (A)	16. (B)	17. (C)	18. (A)	19. (B)	20. (D)
21. (C)	22. (C)	23. (B)	24. (C)	25. (B)					

HOTS (ACHIEVERS SECTION)

26. (B)	27. (C)	28. (A)	29. (B)	30. (C)

2. WORDS AND THEIR MEANINGS

Answer Key

1. (A)	2. (C)	3. (D)	4. (D)	5. (B)	6. (C)	7. (A)	8. (C)	9 (D)	10. (A)
11. (C)	12. (A)	13. (A)	14. (C)	15. (D)					

HOTS (ACHIEVERS SECTION)

16. (B)	17. (A)	18. (D)	19. (D)	20. (C)

3. WORDS AND THEIR OPPOSITES

Answer Key

Fast – Slow	Open – Close	Happy – Sad	Hot – Cold
Old – Young	Bitter – Sweet	Hard – Soft	Healthy – Unhealthy
Heavy – Light	Inside – Outside	Noisy – Silent	Sharp – Blunt
Right – Wrong	Up – Down	Empty – Full	Straight – Bent
		One – Many	

HOTS (ACHIEVERS SECTION)

1. TAKE	2. BALD	3. DARK	4. PRESENT	5. AFTER

Answer Key

1. Masculine	2. Feminine	3. Masculine	4. Masculine	5. Feminine
6. Feminine	7. Masculine	8. Feminine	9. Feminine	10. Feminine
11. Masculine	12. Masculine	13. Feminine	14. Masculine	15. Masculine
16. Feminine	17. Feminine			

HOTS (ACHIEVERS SECTION)

18. Grandmother	19. Policewoman	20. Washerwoman	21. Princess	22. Lioness

5. WORD PAIRS AND ODD ONE OUT

Answer Key

1. Fork	2. Oranges	3. Flower Pot	4. Arrow	5. Thread
6. Bees	7. Ball	8. Pan	9. Socks	10. Nail
11. Moon	12. Key	13. Wife	14. Pencil	15. Girl
16. (A)	17. (B)	18. (B)	19. (C)	20. (D)
21. (A)	22. (B)	23. (C)	24. (C)	25. (A)

HOTS (ACHIEVERS SECTION)

26. Pepper	27. Butter/Jam	28. Dogs	29. (A)	30. (B)

6. ANIMALS AND THEIR YOUNG ONES

Answer Key

1. Nestling	2. Eaglet	3. Fry	4. Pup	5. Tadpole
6. Gosling	7. Cygnet	8. Owlet	9. Cub	10. Pup
11. Pup	12. Calf	13. Poult	14. Foal	15. Kit

HOTS (ACHIEVERS SECTION)

16. Chick	17. Lamb	18. Foal	19. Duckling	20. Fawn

Answer Key

1. Place	2. Thing	3. Person	4. Person	5. Animal
6. Place	7. Place	8. Person	9. Thing	10. Animal
11. Animal	12. Thing	13. Place	14. Person	15. Animal
16. Herd	17. Flock	18. Army	19. Length	20. Strength

HOTS (ACHIEVERS SECTION)

21. boy, man, road	22. bird, nest, house	23. teacher, school
24. robbers, money, jewellery, safe	25. malaria, mosquito	

8. PRONOUN

Answer Key

I				
1. (C)	2. (B)	3. (A)	4. (D)	5. (B)

II

6. **It** is brown.
7. **She** is a teacher.
8. **It** is ringing.
9. **They** are flying kites.
10. **It** is ringing.
11. **We** are going to a birthday party.
12. **She** likes to dance.
13. **It** is the king of the jungle.
14. **He** is my neighbour.
15. The dog was happy when we played with **it**.

HOTS (ACHIEVERS SECTION)

16. (C)	17. (A)	18. (D)	19. (B)	20. (D)

9. VERBS

Answer Key

1. went	2. struck	3. fell, broke	4. sat	5. ran
6. climbed	7. sang, played	8. likes, likes	9. helped, clean	10. wraps
11. threw	12. helped, clean	13. sat	14. brush, take, eat	15. reads
16. bring				

HOTS (ACHIEVERS SECTION)

17. (A), (C)	18. (C), (D)	19. (B), (C)	20. (B), (C)	21. (A), (B)
22. (C), (D)	23. (B)	24. (A), (B)	25. (B), (C)	

10. ARTICLES

Answer Key

1. an	2. a	3. a	4. a	5. a, an	6. a	7. an, a	8. an, a	9. a	10. a
11. an, a	12. An, an		13. a, a, a	14. an	15. an, an		16. a	17. a	

HOTS (ACHIEVERS SECTION)

1. A	2. An	3. An	4. A	5. A	6. An	7. A	8. A	9. An	10. An
11. A	12. An	13. A	14. An	15. A	16. An	17. An			

11. PREPOSITIONS

Answer Key

1. (C)	2. (A)	3. (B)	4. (C)	5. (D)	6. (A)	7. (B)	8. (C)	9. (D)	10. (A)

HOTS (ACHIEVERS SECTION)

11. The boy is going under the fence.
12. The girl is coming down the stairs.
13. The children are swimming across the river.
14. The teacher is standing towards the student.
15. The parrot is sitting on the branch.

12. ADJECTIVES

Answer Key

1. (D)	2. (B)	3. (A)	4. (C)	5. (B)	6. (D)	7. (C)	8. (A)	9. (D)	10. (B)

HOTS (ACHIEVERS SECTION)

11. The packet is very heavy. (heavy/young).

12. Delhi is a big city. (round/big).

13. Respecting elders is a good habit. (good/bad).

14. When it rains, the road gets muddy. (dry/muddy).

13. COMPREHENSION

Answer Key

1. Three	2. Red	3. Chew	4. Ran after it	5. Played

6. grass and pass; drive and hive; funny and honey; tree and me

7. a hive

8. (D) Rob	9. (B) Kim	10. Bill	11. Cowbell

12. (A) Beth (B) Rob (C) Kim (D) Jim (e) Bill

13. Beth does not know what to play.

14. Beth found a cowbell in the box.

14. SPOKEN AND WRITTEN EXPRESSION; PUNCTUATION

Answer Key

1. (C)	2. (D)	3. (C)	4. (A)	5. (C)	6. (C)	7. (C)	8. (C)	9. (C)	10. (B)
11. (B)	12. (B)	13. (D)	14. (A)	15. (C)	16. (C)	17. (B)	18. (C)	19. (B)	20. (A)

HOTS (ACHIEVERS SECTION)

21. (A)	22. (A)	23. (A)	24. (D)	25. (C)	26. (A)	27. (B)	28. (B)	29. (C)	30. (A)

Answer Key

Word and Structure Knowledge

1. (C)	2. (B)	3. (C)	4. (D)	5. (A)	6. (B)	7. WOMAN	8. Both (B) and (C)	9. FLOAT

Reading

10. (D) 11. (A) 12. (C) 13. (B)

Spoken and Written Expression

14. (A) 15. (B)

1. STUDENT NAME (IN ENGLISH CAPITAL LETTERS ONLY)

Students must write and darken the respective circles completely using HB Pencil only. Othewise their Answer Sheets will not be evaluated.

PERSONAL DETAILS

2. SCHOOL CODE

3. CLASS

4. SECTION

5. ROLL NO.

6. QUESTION PAPER SET

A ○
B ○
C ○
D ○

7. MOBILE NUMBER

MARK YOUR ANSWERS

1.	Ⓐ Ⓑ Ⓒ Ⓓ	26.	Ⓐ Ⓑ Ⓒ Ⓓ
2.	Ⓐ Ⓑ Ⓒ Ⓓ	27.	Ⓐ Ⓑ Ⓒ Ⓓ
3.	Ⓐ Ⓑ Ⓒ Ⓓ	28.	Ⓐ Ⓑ Ⓒ Ⓓ
4.	Ⓐ Ⓑ Ⓒ Ⓓ	29.	Ⓐ Ⓑ Ⓒ Ⓓ
5.	Ⓐ Ⓑ Ⓒ Ⓓ	30.	Ⓐ Ⓑ Ⓒ Ⓓ
6.	Ⓐ Ⓑ Ⓒ Ⓓ	31.	Ⓐ Ⓑ Ⓒ Ⓓ
7.	Ⓐ Ⓑ Ⓒ Ⓓ	32.	Ⓐ Ⓑ Ⓒ Ⓓ
8.	Ⓐ Ⓑ Ⓒ Ⓓ	33.	Ⓐ Ⓑ Ⓒ Ⓓ
9.	Ⓐ Ⓑ Ⓒ Ⓓ	34.	Ⓐ Ⓑ Ⓒ Ⓓ
10.	Ⓐ Ⓑ Ⓒ Ⓓ	35.	Ⓐ Ⓑ Ⓒ Ⓓ
11.	Ⓐ Ⓑ Ⓒ Ⓓ	36.	Ⓐ Ⓑ Ⓒ Ⓓ
12.	Ⓐ Ⓑ Ⓒ Ⓓ	37.	Ⓐ Ⓑ Ⓒ Ⓓ
13.	Ⓐ Ⓑ Ⓒ Ⓓ	38.	Ⓐ Ⓑ Ⓒ Ⓓ
14.	Ⓐ Ⓑ Ⓒ Ⓓ	39.	Ⓐ Ⓑ Ⓒ Ⓓ
15.	Ⓐ Ⓑ Ⓒ Ⓓ	40.	Ⓐ Ⓑ Ⓒ Ⓓ
16.	Ⓐ Ⓑ Ⓒ Ⓓ	41.	Ⓐ Ⓑ Ⓒ Ⓓ
17.	Ⓐ Ⓑ Ⓒ Ⓓ	42.	Ⓐ Ⓑ Ⓒ Ⓓ
18.	Ⓐ Ⓑ Ⓒ Ⓓ	43.	Ⓐ Ⓑ Ⓒ Ⓓ
19.	Ⓐ Ⓑ Ⓒ Ⓓ	44.	Ⓐ Ⓑ Ⓒ Ⓓ
20.	Ⓐ Ⓑ Ⓒ Ⓓ	45.	Ⓐ Ⓑ Ⓒ Ⓓ
21.	Ⓐ Ⓑ Ⓒ Ⓓ	46.	Ⓐ Ⓑ Ⓒ Ⓓ
22.	Ⓐ Ⓑ Ⓒ Ⓓ	47.	Ⓐ Ⓑ Ⓒ Ⓓ
23.	Ⓐ Ⓑ Ⓒ Ⓓ	48.	Ⓐ Ⓑ Ⓒ Ⓓ
24.	Ⓐ Ⓑ Ⓒ Ⓓ	49.	Ⓐ Ⓑ Ⓒ Ⓓ
25.	Ⓐ Ⓑ Ⓒ Ⓓ	50.	Ⓐ Ⓑ Ⓒ Ⓓ

8. GENDER

MALE ○
FEMALE ○

9. STREAM

(Only for Class XI and XII Students)

MATHEMATICS ○
BIOLOGY ○
OTHERS ○

Signature of the Student & Date of Examination

Signature of the Invigilator & Date of Examination

V&S Publishers, F-2/16 Ansari Road, Daryaganj, New Delhi-110002, ☎ 011-23240026-27
✉ info@vspublishers.com, 🌐 www.vspublishers.com